SPK
ULTIMATE
COLLECTOR'S
GUIDE VOL. 3

FLOUR

by Jenne Simon

SCHOLASTIC INC.

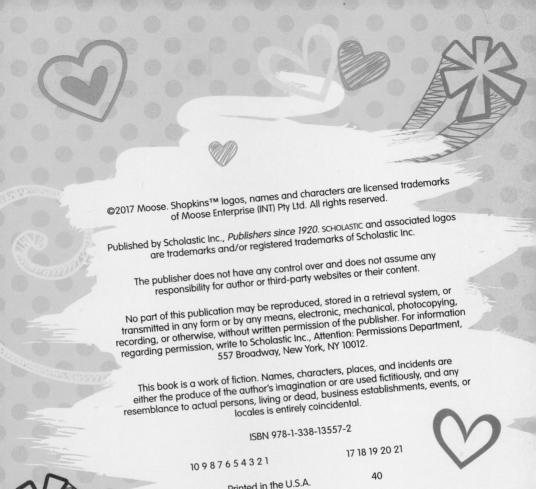

Published by Scholastic Inc., Publishers since 1920. SCHOLASTIC and associated logos are trademarks and/or registered trademarks of Scholastic Inc.

The publisher does not have any control over and does not assume any responsibility for author or third-party websites or their content.

No part of this publication may be reproduced, stored in a retrieval system, or transmitted in any form or by any means, electronic, mechanical, photocopying, recording, or otherwise, without written permission of the publisher. For information regarding permission, write to Scholastic Inc., Attention: Permissions Department, 557 Broadway, New York, NY 10012.

This book is a work of fiction. Names, characters, places, and incidents are either the produce of the author's imagination or are used fictitiously, and any resemblance to actual persons, living or dead, business establishments, events, or locales is entirely coincidental.

ISBN 978-1-338-13557-2

10 9 8 7 6 5 4 3 2 1   17 18 19 20 21

Printed in the U.S.A.   40

First printing 2017

Book design by Erin McMahon
and Ben Mautner

TABLE OF CONTENTS

WELCOME TO SHOPVILLE, THE HOME OF ALL YOUR FAVORITE SHOPKINS™!

This third edition of the Shopkins Ultimate Collector's Guide is full of all the latest characters—including seasons 5 and 6! Stroll down every aisle to learn more about Kooky Cookie, Buncho Bananas, Freda Fern, and many, many more! And don't forget to check out the collector's shopping list in the back of the book to keep track of your favorite characters. Check ya later!

♥AISLE 1♥
ALWAYS FRESH!

The produce aisle is the perfect place to play! The fruit and veggie Shopkins who hang out here know how to have a good time. They're bursting with personality, and there isn't a bad apple in the bunch!

FRUIT & VEG

FAVORITE COLOR:
GRANNY SMITH GREEN

PERSONALITY:
SWEET, TART, AND
A BIT SAUCY

**SIGNATURE DANCE
MOVE:**
THE WORM

**FAVORITE VACATION
DESTINATION:**
MOUNT FUJI

FAVORITE WEATHER:
A CRISP FALL DAY

FIRST MEMORY:
SPROUTING FROM JUST
A WEE LITTLE SEED

Apple Blossom

At her core, Apple Blossom
is sweet as pie and always up
for adventure—she's ready to
take a bite out of life!

QUOTE:
"Check me out!"

PAPA TOMATO

FAVORITE PASTIME:
CHATTING WITH PALS ON THE VINE

AGE:
LET'S JUST SAY HE'S RIPE!

PRIZED POSSESSION:
FAMILY HEIRLOOMS

KNOWN FOR:
BEING A SEASONED STORYTELLER

BEST FRIEND:
GRAN JAM

LIKES:
DARK, DAMP PLACES

HOBBIES:
DIRT—BIKE RACING AND MAKING MUD PIES

FAVORITE VACATION MEMORY:
ANTIQUE SHOPPING ON PORTOBELLO ROAD

BAD HABIT:
SHE CAN SOMETIMES HAVE A BIG HEAD.

QUOTE:
"THERE'S A FUNGUS AMONG US!"

MISS MUSHY MOO

JUICY ORANGE

LIKES:
JUICY SECRETS

DISLIKES:
RHYMING!

KNOWN FOR:
HER PITHY JOKES

SPORTS SKILL:
THE SQUEEZE PLAY

QUOTE:
"I'M JUICED UP AND
READY TO GO!"

LIKES:
PUZZLES AND MAIZES

PRIZED POSSESSION:
SILK PAJAMAS

**SIGNATURE
DANCE MOVE:**
POP—AND—LOCK

FAVORITE COLOR:
BUTTER YELLOW

BEST FEATURE:
HIS HUSKY VOICE

CORNY COB

Strawberry Kiss

When Strawberry Kiss isn't lost in a daydream, you're sure to find her working on a new poem. Here's one she's just finished! *Roses are red, violets are blue, Shopkins are sweet, and so are you!*

FAVORITE HOLIDAY:
VALENTINE'S DAY

BEST FRIEND:
APPLE BLOSSOM

FAVORITE SONG:
"STRAWBERRY FIELDS FOREVER"

LIKES:
PINK LEMONADE

FAVORITE SINGER:
BERRY MANILOW

DREAMS ABOUT:
WHAT'S IN THE STRAW—BERRY PATCH AT THE END OF THE RAINBOW

PERSONALITY:
SWEET, BUT A LITTLE SPOILED

FAVORITE ANIMAL:
PARTRIDGE

PERFECT ACCESSORY:
HER PINK "PEAR" OF SUNGLASSES

BEST FRIEND:
LIPPY LIPS

QUOTE:
"I CAN'T HELP IT IF I HAVE APPEAL."

POSH PEAR

BEST VACATION MEMORY:
A LUAU IN HAWAII

CAN'T GET ENOUGH OF:
FUN IN THE SUN

HOBBIES:
SUNBAKING AND HANGING TEN

FAVORITE WEATHER:
A TROPICAL BREEZE

KNOWN FOR:
HER GOLDEN OUTLOOK ON LIFE

PINEAPPLE CRUSH

LIMITED EDITION

LENNY LIME

KNOWN FOR:
HIS CONCENTRATION

FAVORITE COLOR:
CITRON

BEST FRIEND:
SOUR LEMON

FAVORITE VACATION DESTINATION:
THE FLORIDA KEYS

QUOTE:
"PUCKER UP!"

HOBBY:
LEAFING THROUGH THE NEWSPAPER

BAD HABIT:
STALKING OUT OF A ROOM WHEN SHE'S ANGRY

BEST FRIEND:
ROCKIN' BROC

PERSONAL HERO:
FLORETS NIGHTINGALE

QUOTE:
"LET'S VEG OUT!"

CHLOE FLOWER

NICKNAME:
THE POD SQUAD

BEST FRIEND:
CHERRIE TOMATOES

GREATEST FEAR:
BEING ALONE

FAVORITE HOBBY:
JUGGLING

QUOTE:
"GIVE PEAS
A CHANCE!"

SWEET PEA

PERSONALITY:
SWEET AS PIE

KNOWN FOR:
HER FUZZY MEMORY

HANGOUT:
THE BALL PIT

FAVORITE VACATION
DESTINATION:
GEORGIA

FAVORITE HOBBY:
CHILLING OUT WITH
ICE CREAM DREAM

PEACHY

NICKNAME:
DOUBLE TROUBLE

KNOWN FOR:
FINISHING EACH OTHER'S SENTENCES

FAVORITE COLORS:
BLACK AND RED

BEST FRIEND:
APRIL APRICOT

NICKNAME:
MARASCHINO MAMAS

CHEEKY CHERRIES

APRIL APRICOT

DISLIKES:
WRINKLES

PERSONALITY:
FUN AND FRUITY

SENSE OF HUMOR:
DRY

KNOWN FOR:
ALWAYS GETTING IN A JAM

QUOTE:
"THIS IS THE PITS!"

13

DREAMS ABOUT:
LIVING TO A RIPE
OLD AGE

**SIGNATURE
DANCE MOVE:**
GOING BANANAS

KNOWN FOR:
ALWAYS WEARING
SUNSCREEN. HE PEELS!

**FAVORITE VACATION
DESTINATION:**
ANYWHERE WITH
A HAMMOCK

FAVORITE ANIMAL:
YELLOW LABRADOR

Buncho Bananas

Buncho Bananas may have a thick skin, but inside, he's just a big ol' softie. He loves monkeying around, but never wants to hurt anyone's peelings!

QUOTE:
"Love you bunches!"

KAREN CARROT

HOBBY:
GARDENING

LIKES:
MAKING SNOWMEN

DISLIKES:
GETTING LOST
IN A CROWD

FAVORITE
CHARACTER:
BUGS BUNNY

BEST FEATURE:
HER SHARP EYES

FAVORITE ACCESSORY:
HER WEDGE HEELS

NICKNAME:
SOURPUSS

SIGNATURE DANCE
MOVE:
THE LEMON MERENGUE

KNOWN FOR:
HER ZEST FOR LIFE

QUOTE:
"WHEN LIFE HANDS
YOU LEMONS, MAKE
LEMONADE!"

PIPPA LEMON

BAD HABIT:
TRYING TO TOP EVERYTHING ALL THE TIME

FAVORITE FLOWER:
CHERRY BLOSSOM

FIRST MEMORY:
DOING EVERYTHING WITH HER TWIN SISTER. THEY WERE ATTACHED AT THE STEM!

FAVORITE CARTOON:
TOM AND CHERRY

QUOTE:
"ENJOY THE FRUITS OF YOUR LABOR!"

CHERRY-ANNE

ROS BERRY

FAVORITE COLORS:
BLACK AND BLUE

KNOWN FOR:
GETTING IN AND OUT OF JAMS

BEST FEATURE:
HER RASPY VOICE

NICKNAME:
FRUITY CUTIE

QUOTE:
"HOW BERRYLICIOUS!"

⬤AISLE 2⬤
SMELLS DELICIOUS!

The Bakery aisle is always warm and inviting. These well-bread Shopkins make sure to savor the sweeter things in life. Feeling cozy around them is a piece of cake!

BAKERY

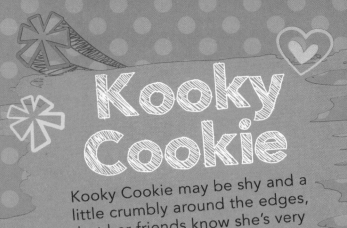

Kooky Cookie

Kooky Cookie may be shy and a little crumbly around the edges, but her friends know she's very well-rounded.

FAVORITE COLORS:
BLACK AND WHITE

SPORTS SKILL:
DUNKING

KNOWN FOR:
MILKING A JOKE

GOOD AT:
THINKING OUTSIDE THE COOKIE JAR

NICKNAME:
SNICKERDOODLE

SECRET TALENT:
FORTUNE-TELLING

"My dad says I'm a chip off the old block!"

DONNA DONUT

HOBBY:
HOLING UP WITH A
GOOD BOOK

FAVORITE WEATHER:
A SPRINKLE OF RAIN

KNOWN FOR:
HAVING DOZENS OF
FRIENDS

FIRST MEMORY:
POPPING OUT OF
THE OVEN

FAVORITE SONG:
"DOUGH—RE—MI"

FAVORITE MEAL:
BRUNCH

BEST TIME OF DAY:
MORNING. SHE'S AN
EARLY RISER!

SPORTS SKILL:
YOGA, ESPECIALLY THE
SUNRISE SALUTATION

BEST FRIEND:
SPILT MILK

QUOTE:
"TODAY IS A
BRAN—NEW DAY!"

MINI MUFFIN

Slick Breadstick

PERSONALITY:
HE'S CRUSTY ON THE OUTSIDE BUT WARM ON THE INSIDE. IT'S A TALL ORDER BEING A BREADSTICK!

FAVORITE HANGOUT
A PARISIAN CAFÉ

DISLIKES:
RAIN—IT MAKES HIM FEEL SOGGY.

BEST FRIENDS:
ALPHA SOUP AND FASTA PASTA

QUOTE:
"Zer is always time for ze café break, no?"

KNOWN FOR:
HIS DRY SENSE OF HUMOR

HOBBY:
BUTTERING UP HIS FRIENDS

BEST FRIEND:
LANA BANANA BREAD

FAVORITE COLOR:
WHITE

GOOD AT:
RISING TO THE OCCASION

SPORTS SKILLS:
PUTTING SOME SLICE ON
A TENNIS BALL

QUOTE:
"IF IT'S GETTING TOO HOT,
IT'S TIME TO POP!"

TOASTIE BREAD

BAGEL BILLY

KNOWN FOR:
LAYING IT ON THICK

FAVORITE WEATHER:
BAKING IN THE HEAT

PERSONALITY:
BAGELICIOUS

**SIGNATURE
DANCE MOVE:**
ROUNDHOUSE KICK

LIKES:
EVERYTHING

FAVORITE SONG:
"ROLL OVER, BEETHOVEN"

QUOTE:
"OPEN SESAME!"

SIGNATURE
DANCE MOVE:
RAISIN' THE ROOF

KNOWN FOR:
GETTING TO THE ROOT
OF A PROBLEM

PERSONALITY:
SWEET BUT A
LITTLE NUTTY

PRIZED POSSESSION:
HER 14-CARROT
GOLD RING

QUOTE:
"AS LONG AS YOU HAVE
FRIENDS, EVERYTHING ELSE
IS JUST FROSTING."

CARRIE CARROT CAKE

MARY MERINGUE

KNOWN FOR:
WHIPPING UP TREATS

BAD HABIT:
HER SWEET TOOTH

PERSONALITY:
SHE ALWAYS HAS HER
HEAD IN THE CLOUDS.

SECRET WEAPON:
A DOLLOP OF COURAGE

HOMETOWN:
BORN AND RAISED
IN ALASKA

D'Lish Donut

D'Lish Donut is the sportiest Shopkin around. She has a competitive spirit and always shoots for the perfect hole in one!

FAVORITE SPORT:
GOLF

BEST FRIEND:
CHEEKY CHOCOLATE

LOVES WHEN:
THERE'S A LIGHT FROSTING OF SNOW ON THE GROUND.

BAD HABIT:
FRITTERING THE DAY AWAY

HOBBY:
GLAZING POTTERY

FAVORITE COLOR:
CINNAMON BROWN

QUOTE:
"I dough know what I'd do without my friends!"

CHEESE LOUISE

PERSONALITY:
SHE MAY BE RICH, BUT
SHE'S VERY SWEET.

KNOWN FOR:
HER NEW YORK STYLE

GOOD AT:
TELLING CHEESY JOKES

FAVORITE COLOR:
CHOCOLATE BROWN

QUOTE:
"LIFE IS A CAKEWALK!"

LIKES:
BIRTHDAY PARTIES

DISLIKES:
SHARING

BEST FRIEND:
CUPCAKE QUEEN

NICKNAME:
CRUMBS

QUOTE:
"THAT'S THE ICING
ON THE CAKE!"

PATTY CAKE

Bread Head

PERSONALITY:
THIS CHATTERBOX IS INDEPENDENT AND CONFIDENT—HE ALWAYS HAS IT IN THE BAG!

LIKES:
SAVING HIS DOUGH

DISLIKES:
STALE JOKES

FAVORITE ACCESSORY:
LOAFERS

GREATEST FEAR:
GETTING SANDWICHED IN A TIGHT SPACE

Creamy Cookie Cupcake

An all-around sweetheart, Creamy Cookie Cupcake is a smooth operator who makes mixing good ideas look like a piece of cake!

PERSONALITY:
DON'T CALL HER VANILL

SIGNATURE DANCE MOVE:
THE SHAKE AND BAKE

FUTURE GOAL:
TO BECOME A WRAPPE

BAD HABIT:
SHE'S A CHOCOHOLIC!

LIKES:
SWEET DREAMS

QUOTE:
"That's the way the cookie crumbles!"

DOLLY DONUT

GREATEST FEAR:
BEAR CLAWS

KNOWN FOR:
THE GLAZED LOOK
IN HER EYES

FAVORITE MOVIE:
THE DIRTY DOZEN

SPORTS SKILL:
SKIING ON FRESHLY
FALLEN POWDER

QUOTE:
"I DOUGH NOT LIKE
TO GOSSIP!"

PERSONALITY:
REGAL

KNOWN FOR:
HER FROSTING IS HER
CROWNING GLORY.

**FAVORITE VACATION
DESTINATION:**
KINGSTON, JAMAICA

NICKNAME:
YOUR HIGHNESS

**FAVORITE
ACCESSORY:**
TIARA

ROYAL CUPCAKE

PERSONALITY:
SOFT-CENTERED

HOBBY:
WATCHING MUSHY MOVIES

FAVORITE VILLAIN:
THE WICKED WITCH
OF THE WEST

DISLIKES:
FEELING SANDWICHED
BETWEEN A ROCK AND
A HARD PLACE

FAVORITE WEATHER:
MELTINGLY HOT

FASHION STYLE:
HER TOP AND BOTTOM
ALWAYS MATCH!

Mel T Moment

Mel T Moment feels things deeply. She's got hidden layers, and the sweetest gesture will melt her heart!

QUOTE:

"With the Shopkins around, there's never a dull moment!"

28

♡ AISLE 3 ♡
WHAT'S COOKIN?

The seasoned Shopkins in the pantry aisle are full of flavor. But watch out! Some of them can be a bit wild. They like to spice things up!

PANTRY & INTERNATIONAL FOODS

Gran Jam

This caring mama watches over all of Shopville. She spreads love and slathers affection on the Shopkins, sweetening their lives with her kind words.

FAVORITE COLOR
RASPBERRY PINK

HOBBIES:
KNITTING AND JAMMI
ON THE UKULELE

SIGNATURE DANCE MOVE:
THE JELLY ROLL

KNOWN FOR:
PRESERVING MEMORIES
HER SCRAPBOOK

HERO:
ALEXANDER THE GRAP

BAD HABIT:
STEWING IN HER
OWN JUICES

QUOTE:
"Aren't you a little sweetie?"

HER FRIENDS SAY:
"SALLY SHAKES ADDS
FLAVOR TO LIFE!"

DISLIKES:
UNSAVORY CHARACTERS

SPORTS SKILL:
THE PINCH HIT

HOBBY:
ROCK CLIMBING

FAVORITE BAND:
THE SPICED GIRLS

SALLY SHAKES

KNOWS HOW TO:
SHAKE IT ON THE
DANCE FLOOR

WISHES HE:
COULD STOP SNEEZING!

COUSINS:
JALAPENO, CAYENNE,
AND PAPRIKA

BEST FRIEND:
SALLY SHAKES. THEY'RE
RARELY SEEN APART.

QUOTE:
"LET'S SPICE THINGS UP!"

PEPPE PEPPER

HONEEEY

HOBBIES:
THE SPELLING BEE AND CATCHING FLIES

GREATEST FEAR:
GETTING HIVES

BEST FRIEND:
LEE TEA

LOVES TO:
COMB THE PAGES OF A GOOD MAGAZINE

QUOTE:
"WHAT'S THE BUZZ?"

KNOWN FOR:
BEING A BIT OF A MESS

LIKES:
HALF—BAKED IDEAS

DISLIKES:
ROLLING PINS AND FEELING SCATTERED

FAVORITE ACCESSORY:
HER POWDER COMPACT

QUOTE:
"FLOUR POWER!"

FI FI FLOUR

Breaky Crunch

Breaky Crunch wakes up at the crack of dawn each morning and heads to the gym. Lifting weights and getting in a few crunches is the perfect way to start his day!

HOBBIES:
BOWLING AND STAYING IN SHAPE

PERSONALITY:
HE GOES AGAINST THE GRAIN

LIKES:
SURPRISE GIFTS

BEST FRIEND:
SPILT MILK

DISLIKES:
FLAKES

GREATEST FEAR:
GETTING SOGGY

QUOTE:
"Nothing can box me up!"

33

LIKES:
HANDBAGS, SHOULDER
BAGS, AND TEA BAGS!

DISLIKES:
STEEP PRICES

FAVORITE ANIMAL:
TEACUP PIG

FAVORITE COLORS:
BLACK AND GREEN

QUOTE:
"I SMELL TROUBLE
BREWING!"

LIMITED EDITION

LEE TEA

PERSONALITY:
SWEET, BUT NEVER
ARTIFICIAL

FAVORITE COLORS:
BROWN AND WHITE

LIKES:
REFINED MANNERS

SECRET TALENT:
BEING ORGANIZED.
STORAGE CUBES ARE
HER THING!

QUOTE:
"THERE'S NOTHING
SWEETER THAN
FRIENDSHIP."

SUGAR LUMP

FASTA PASTA

FAVORITE ACCESSORY:
HIS BOW TIE

HOBBY:
NOODLING AROUND ON
THE PIANO

PRIZED POSSESSION:
HIS LUCKY "PENNE"

SECRET WEAPON:
ELBOW GREASE

PERSONAL HERO:
HIS UNCLE ALFREDO

FAVORITE SONG:
"ROE, ROE, ROE
YOUR BOAT"

LIKES:
SWIMMING UPSTREAM

DISLIKES:
CANNED APPLAUSE

FAVORITE CHARACTER:
THE TIN MAN

QUOTE:
"SOMETHING'S FISHY!"

LIMITED EDITION

TIN'A'TUNA

35

TOMMY KETCHUP

FAVORITE COLOR:
TOMATO RED

DISLIKES:
FEELING DRAINED

NICKNAME:
SQUIRT

BEST FRIEND:
FRANK FURTER

LIKES:
ZESTY DEBATES

MAIN RIVAL:
CORNELL MUSTARD

QUOTE:
"WAIT, GUYS! LET ME CATCH UP!"

PERSONALITY:
A LITTLE BIT CRUNCHY

FAVORITE VACATION DESTINATION:
CANCÚN, MEXICO

FAVORITE WEATHER:
HOT! HOT! HOT!

HOBBY:
SALSA DANCING

BAD HABIT:
FALLING APART UNDER PRESSURE

QUOTE:
"AY, CARAMBA!"

TACO TERRIE

FAVORITE VACATION DESTINATION:
ROME, ITALY

NICKNAME:
MEATBALL

BEST FRIEND:
SAUSAGE SIZZLE

BAD HABIT:
SLURPING HER FOOD

SECRET TALENT:
TWIRLING IN BALLET CLASS

NETTI SPAGHETTI

WALLY WATER

FAVORITE COLOR
AQUA

BAD HABIT:
HE CAN GET BOILING MAD

NICKNAME:
H_2O

SIGNATURE DANCE MOVE:
THE SPRINKLER

FAVORITE HANGOUT:
CHILLING AT THE POOL

Miss Sprinkles

PERSONALITY:
LIGHT AND LIVELY

FAVORITE COLOR:
RAINBOW—SHE
LIKES THEM ALL!

BEST FRIEND:
LITTLE CHOC BOTTLE

**FAVORITE TIME
OF DAY:**
DESSERT TIME

FASHION STYLE:
THE BRIGHTER, THE BETTER!

FAVORITE ANIMAL:
UNICORN

Miss Sprinkles is always ready to party—she makes every gathering brighter, happier, and way more fun!

QUOTE:

"Everyone needs a sprinkle of sunshine in their lives!"

PERSONALITY:
SHE CAN BE A BIT
OF A FLAKE.

BEST FRIEND:
MAVIS MAPLE SYRUP

FASHION STYLE:
NATURAL AND
UNBLEACHED

KNOWN FOR:
ALWAYS GETTING
THE SCOOOP

FAVORITE FLOWER:
WHITE LILY

FLEUR FLOUR

CASSIE CASTER SUGAR

PERSONALITY:
A REAL SWEETHEART

FAVORITE GAME:
CANDY LAND

DISLIKES:
ANYTHING ARTIFICIAL

FASHION STYLE:
SUPER FINE

QUOTE:
"LIFE IS SWEET!"

FREDDY FRIED RICE

FAVORITE MUSIC:
WOK 'N' ROLL

BEST FRIEND:
JASMINE RICE

PERSONALITY:
HOT—TEMPERED

FAVORITE VACATION DESTINATION:
CHINA

QUOTE:
"RICE TO MEET YOU!"

KNOWN FOR:
SAUCY JOKES

NICKNAME:
SALTY DOG

LIKES:
SAVORING THE MOMENT

DISLIKES:
GETTING PUSHED TO THE SIDE

QUOTE:
"I'M SOY HAPPY!"

SAM SOY

● AISLE 4 ●
COOL AND CREAMY!

This is the aisle where everyone in Shopville likes to kick back and chill out. All are welcome—the dairy and frozen food Shopkins don't give anyone the cold shoulder!

DAIRY & ♡
FROZEN FOOD

Chee Zee

Chee Zee has a secret talent—he writes original rap songs! Check out his latest beats: My name is Chee Zee, I'm bold and breezy, but don't try to squeeze me, or else I'll get freezy!

LIKES:
TAKING CENTER STAGE

FAVORITE SCARY MOVIE:
FRANKENSTEIN'S MUENSTER

BEST FRIENDS:
FREEZY PEAZY AND CHEEZEY B

FAVORITE VACATIO DESTINATION:
THE SWISS ALPS

HIS FRIENDS SAY
"CHEE ZEE CAN BE A CRACKERS."

GREATEST FEAR:
MICE

QUOTE:
"Gouda been better. Let's try it again!"

FAVORITE WEATHER:
SNOW

FIRST MEMORY:
LEAVING THE POD

PET PEEVE:
BAD MANNERS. HE
MINDS HIS P'S
AND Q'S.

FAVORITE RAPPER:
MASTER P

Freezy Peazy

This Mr. Ice Guy is a bagful of laughs—and he's always the first one there when someone gets hurt.

QUOTE:
"Be cool!"

Buttercup

SECRET TALENT:
HE HAS GREAT TASTE!

FIRST MEMORY:
BEING WHIPPED
INTO SHAPE

FAVORITE COLOR:
MELLOW YELLOW

PERSONALITY:
RICH, BUT NEVER SPOILED

HIS FRIENDS SAY:
"BUTTERCUP WILL MELT
YOUR HEART!"

Buttercup can be a little salty
sometimes, but he always sticks
by his friends!

LIMITED
EDITION

BUT

44

LOVES TO:
CHILL OUT

FUN FACT:
RUMOR HAS IT SHE
HAS A TWIN.

HOBBIES:
ICE-SKATING AND
SLEDDING!

GREATEST FEAR:
FREEZER BURN

QUOTE:
"I CAN LICK
ANY PROBLEM!"

POPSI COOL

YO-CHI

HOBBY:
SWIRLING AROUND THE
DANCE FLOOR

**FAVORITE POP
MUSIC ARTIST:**
VANILLA ICE CREAM

PERSONALITY:
WELL-CULTURED

FASHION STYLE:
SHE'S ALWAYS SPORTING
A NEW TOPPING!

QUOTE:
"EVERY DAY SHOULD HAVE
A DIFFERENT FLAVOR!"

4

Spilt Milk

You'll never be bored with Spilt Milk around! He's half silly and half serious, and he really likes to stir things up!

KNOWN FOR:
BEING A BIT OF A KLUTZ

FAVORITE WEATHER:
POURING RAIN

HOBBY:
SKIMMING THROUGH COMIC BOOKS

DISLIKES:
SPOILED PEOPLE REALLY GET HIM STEAMED!

FAVORITE VACATION DESTINATION:
WISCONSIN

PERSONALITY:
HE SOMETIMES CRIES OVER LITTLE THINGS

BEST JOKE:
"What do you get from an Alaskan cow? Ice cream!"

BERRY TUBS

PERSONALITY:
BERRY, BERRY NICE

FAVORITE
ACCESSORY:
RASPBERRY BERET

PET PEEVE:
PUTTING THE CARTON
BEFORE THE HORSE

FAVORITE VILLAIN:
MR. FREEZE

QUOTE:
"I'M A SHER—BET!"

FASHION STYLE:
A LITTLE PLAIN

FAVORITE WEEKEND
ACTIVITY:
SUNDAE SCHOOL

DISLIKES:
ROCKY ROADS

FAVORITE JOKE:
HOW DO ASTRONAUTS EAT
ICE CREAM? IN FLOATS!

QUOTE:
"HOW HAVE YOU BEAN?"

V. NILLA TUBS

● AISLE 5 ●
IT'S PARTY TIME!

There's always a reason to celebrate with these rockin' Shopkins. Whether it's someone's birthday, a holiday, or just an average Tuesday, they'll find something that deserves a special treat!

PARTY FOOD & SWEET TREATS

RAINBOW BITE

STYLE SECRET:
ANY COLOR LOOKS GOOD ON HER.

BEST FRIEND:
SODA POPS

PROFESSIONAL HERO:
ROY G. BIV

HOBBIES:
PAINTING

QUOTE:
"YOU NEED A LITTLE RAIN TO GET A RAINBOW!"

PERSONALITY:
SUPER BUBBLY

DISLIKES:
BEING SHAKEN UP

BAD HABIT:
TOO MUCH CAFFEINE

HOBBY:
REFRESHING HER WARDROBE

QUOTE:
"I HATE TO BURST YOUR BUBBLE . . ."

SODA POPS

WISHES

AGE:
A YEAR WORTH
CELEBRATING!

PRIZED POSSESSION:
CANDLES FROM HER
FIRST BIRTHDAY

FAVORITE SONG:
"WHEN YOU WISH UPON
A STAR"

KNOWN FOR:
THROWING SURPRISE
PARTIES

QUOTE:
"YOU *CAN* HAVE YOUR
CAKE AND EAT IT, TOO!"

LIKES:
WIGGLING TO A
GOOD BEAT

FAVORITE SONG:
"GETTING JIGGLY WITH IT"

PERSONALITY:
A WORRIER WHO
BOUNCES FROM
PROBLEM TO PROBLEM

PET PEEVE:
IT FEELS LIKE HER
FRIENDS CAN SEE RIGHT
THROUGH HER.

MOTTO:
DANCING SHAKES THE
STRESS AWAY

WOBBLES

PERSONALITY:
SWEET, BUT A LITTLE
HARD TO GET
ALONG WITH

BAD HABIT:
SHE'S STUCK IN
HER WAYS.

DISLIKES:
LOLLYGAGGIN' AROUND

BEST FRIEND:
CANDI COTTON

QUOTE:
"I'M NO SUCKER!"

LOLLI POPPINS

BUBBLES

LIKES:
A GOOD CHAT-'N'-CHEW
WITH FRIENDS

KNOWN FOR:
BURSTING INTO SONG

SPORTS SKILL:
POP FLY

BAD HABIT:
FLAPPING HER GUMS

**FAVORITE MOVIE
CHARACTER:**
CHEWBACCA

BEST PRANK:
CONVINCING HER FRIENDS
SHE'S MELTED

BEST FRIENDS:
D'LISH DONUT AND
APPLE BLOSSOM

FAVORITE ANIMAL:
CHOCOLATE LABORADOR

**FAVORITE VACATION
DESTINATION:**
HERSHEY, PENNSYLVANIA

KNOWN FOR:
BREAKING OUT LAUGHING

HOBBIES:
PULLING PRANKS AND
MELTING HEARTS

Cheeky Chocolate

Cheeky Chocolate loves to laugh.
She's a prankster who isn't afraid
of getting her hands dirty!

QUOTE:
"Oops! I spilled the beans!"

ICE CREAM DREAM

BEST FRIEND:
WAFFLE SUE

PET PEEVE:
BRAIN FREEZE!

PERSONALITY:
SHE CAN BE A
BIT DRIPPY.

NICKNAME:
HALF-PINT

PRIZED POSSESSION:
A STERLING SILVER SCOOP

HER FRIENDS SAY:
"SHE'S A REAL SOFTIE!"

BEST FRIEND:
CHOCO LAVA

DISLIKES:
BEING TOO HOT,
IT MAKES HER FEEL PUFFY.

LOVES TO:
TELL STORIES BY
THE CAMPFIRE

QUOTE:
"LET'S PLAY 'S'MORE!"

LIMITED EDITION

MARSHA MELLOW

EARLIEST MEMORY:
BEING JUST A WEE
SHOPKIN IN A SNUGGLY
WRAPPER

PERSONALITY:
SHE'S FULL OF SURPRISES.

BAD HABIT:
SPONGING OFF HER
FRIENDS

DISLIKES:
NEEDING FILLINGS AT
THE DENTIST

QUOTE:
"SHOPKINS ARE THE
CREAM OF THE CROP!"

TWINKY WINKS

LIMITED EDITION

LE'QUORICE

PERSONALITY:
SOME SAY SHE'S AN
ACQUIRED TASTE

FAVORITE GAME:
HOPSCOTCH

HER FRIENDS KNOW:
SHE'LL ALWAYS STICK
BY THEM.

FASHION STYLE:
COLORFUL LAYERS

BEST FRIEND:
MANDY CANDY

CUPCAKE QUEEN

FAVORITE COLOR:
BUTTERCREAM

ENJOYS:
HOSTING GRAND BALLS

FAVORITE ACCESSORY:
A CROWN OF FROSTING

PRIZED POSSESSION:
RED—VELVET SLIPPERS

DREAMS ABOUT:
BECOMING ROYALTY

HOBBY:
GOING TO THE MOVIES

SPORTS SKILL:
NONE—SHE'S A REAL
BUTTERFINGERS!

**HAS A
TENDENCY TO:**
POP UP UNEXPECTEDLY

QUOTE:
"I'VE GOT THIS
IN THE BAG!"

POPPY CORN

Suzie Sundae

Suzie Sundae is a Shopkin with a lot of glass! And if you want to have fun, there's no topping a day with Suzie!

FAVORITE MOVIE:
FROZEN

HOBBIES:
RELAXING ON A SUNDA

FAVORITE COLOR:
CHERRY RED

SIGNATURE DANCE MOVE:
THE SPLITS

FAVORITE FOOD:
SHE'S NUTS ABOUT ICE CREAM.

BEST FRIEND:
ICE CREAM DREAM

QUOTE:
"Pretty please ... with a cherry on top?"

PERSONALITY:
ONE COLORFUL CHARACTER

FAVORITE HANGOUT:
SANDWICHED BETWEEN
TWO GOOD FRIENDS

**SIGNATURE DANCE
MOVE:**
PIROUETTE

**FAVORITE VACATION
DESTINATION:**
THE EIFFEL TOWER

QUOTE:
"OOH, LA LA!"

MACCA ROON

CANDY APPLE

PERSONALITY:
DEPENDABLE. SHE'LL
ALWAYS STICK WITH YOU!

FAVORITE HANGOUT:
THE COUNTY FAIR

LIKES:
HAYRIDES AND
MERRY-GO-ROUNDS

KNOWN FOR:
GETTING INTO STICKY
SITUATIONS

GREATEST FEAR:
GOING TO THE DENTIST

LIKES:
SURPRISES

SECRET TALENT:
RAPPING

PERSONALITY:
GIVING

PET PEEVE:
FORGOTTEN BIRTHDAYS

FAVORTE SPORT:
BOXING

FAVORITE ACCESSORY:
RIBBONS AND
BOWS

Miss Pressy

Miss Pressy has a gift for gab. She can keep a secret, but she'll be bursting to let out what's inside.

QUOTE:
"Sharing is caring!"

58

FAVORITE COLOR:
CREAM

BAD HABIT:
WAFFLING ON AND ON

FAVORITE SPORT:
ICE HOCKEY

NICKNAME:
SUGAR

FAVORITE WEATHER:
DRIPPY

KYLIE CONE

PERSONALITY:
COOL AND FRESH

FAVORITE COLOR:
BLUE

BEST FRIEND:
PANCAKE JAKE

HIDDEN TALENT:
CAN BLEND INTO
A CROWD

QUOTE:
"LOOKS LIKE IT'S
SMOOTH SAILING!"

BERRY SMOOTHIE

Pancake Jake

Wake up and say good morning to Pancake Jake! He's a stack of fun and totally pantastic!

LIKES:
READING THE SUNDAY NEWSPAPER

BAD HABIT:
WHEN HE SINGS, HE'S A LITTLE FLAT.

FAVORITE TREE:
MAPLE

FAVORITE VACATION DESTINATION:
VERMONT

FAVORITE CHARACTERS:
FLAPJACK AND JILL

KNOWN FOR:
FLIPPING OVER BACKWARD TO HELP HIS FRIENDS

QUOTE:
"Batter up!"

CUTE FRUIT JELLO

KNOWN FOR:
SHAKING THINGS UP

PERSONALITY:
FRUITY AND FUN

DISLIKES:
SHIVERS

BEST FRIEND:
ICE CREAM KATE

QUOTE:
"I'M TREMBLING
INSIDE!"

PERSONALITY:
ANY WAY YOU SLICE IT,
SHE'S A SWEETIE.

BEST FRIEND:
CHOCKY CROISSANT

FAVORITE COLOR:
PINK, PINK, AND
MORE PINK

HOBBIES:
DECORATING AND DESIGN

QUOTE:
"YOU WANT A
PIECE OF ME?"

SPRINKLE LEE CAKE

Stacks Cookie

Stacks Cookie always makes a sweet first impression. This is one Shopkin with heaps of personality and pizzazz!

FAVORITE SPORT:
LONG, TALL TALES

DISLIKES:
FEELING CRUMBY

FASHION STYLE:
BIG AND TALL

BAD HABIT:
SHE HAS A CHIP ON HER SHOULDER.

QUOTE:

"Don't stay a wafer too long!"

♡ AISLE 6 ♡
SCRUB—A—DUB!

The cleaning and laundry aisle is super fresh. The tidy Shopkins who hang out here make a game out of putting things in order. And they never play dirty!

CLEANING &
LAUNDRY

Molly Mops

This hardworking miss knows how to get the job done. But don't be fooled by her can-do attitude—she's buckets of fun!

SPORTS SKILL:
MOPPING THE FLOOR WITH THE COMPETITION

ENJOYS:
CHECKING THINGS OFF HER BUCKET LIST

FAVORITE SONG:
"WHISTLE WHILE YOU WORK"

LIKES:
SEEING HER REFLECTION IN A CLEAN, SHINY FLOOR

HER FRIENDS SAY:
"MOLLY CAN WRING OUT ANY PROBLEM!"

SECRET TALENT:
GETTING A HANDLE ON THE SITUATION

KNOWN FOR:
HER STRONG WORK ETHIC

FAVORITE SONG:
"WIPEOUT"

SIGNATURE
DANCE MOVE:
THE TOOTSIE ROLL

LIKES TO:
UNWIND WITH A
GOOD MAGAZINE

DISLIKES:
FEELING FLUSHED

QUOTE:
"LET THE GOOD
TIMES ROLL!"

LEAFY

LIMITED
EDITION

RUB—A—GLOVE

KNOWN FOR:
DISHING THE DIRT

HOBBY:
WATER SPORTS

BEST FRIEND:
MOLLY MOPS

PRIZED POSSESSION:
RUBBER DUCK

QUOTE:
"CAN YOU GIVE
ME A HAND?"

PERSONALITY:
HONEST AND CLEAN-CUT

BEST FRIEND:
LEAFY

LIKES:
WATER SLIDES AND
BUBBLE BATHS

SECRET WEAPON:
THE SPARKLE IN HIS EYE

DISLIKES:
AIRING DIRTY LAUNDRY
IN PUBLIC

KNOWN FOR:
CLEANING HOUSE

Squeaky Clean

Squeaky Clean always does what's right. He likes to try new things, but he isn't afraid to clean up after his own messes.

QUOTE:
"Neat-o!"

● AISLE 7 ●
HOME, SWEET HOME!

Welcome to Aisle 7, where the friendly homewares Shopkins are always eager for company! They're sure to make anyone feel right at home.

BABY, HOME AND GARDEN & STATIONERY

AGE:
JUST A TYKE

SECRET TALENT:
KEEPING THE PEACE—
SHE'S A PACIFIER!

FAVORITE SINGER:
LADY GOO-GOO-GA-GA

BEST FRIEND:
SIPPY SIPS

FAVORITE COLOR:
BABY BLUE

FAVORITE FLOWER:
BABY'S BREATH

Dum Mee Mee

Dum Mee Mee is a little cutie who was born to shop. She may be tiny, but she's got a very big heart.

QUOTE:

"You'll never cry when I'm around."

PERSONALITY:
SHE CAN BE RATHER FORMULAIC.

RELAXES BY:
REHEATING IN A NICE, WARM BATH

LIKES:
NURSERY RHYMES

DISLIKES:
PEOPLE WHO BOTTLE UP THEIR EMOTIONS

LOOKS UP TO:
SIPPY SIPS

DRIBBLES

KNOWN FOR:
NEVER SPILLING A SECRET

FAVORITE SPORTING EVENT:
THE WORLD CUP

ENJOYS:
SINGING LULLABIES BEFORE BEDTIME

PRIZED POSSESSION:
A STUFFED BEAR

QUOTE:
"ENJOY LIFE ONE SIP AT A TIME"

SIPPY SIPS

69

LANA LAMP

FAVORITE TIME OF DAY:
BRIGHT AND EARLY

BEST FEATURE:
HER SMILE HAS SERIOUS WATTAGE

PERSONALITY:
BRILLIANT

KNOWN FOR:
ALWAYS LOOKING ON THE BRIGHT SIDE

QUOTE:
"WE'VE GOT IT MADE IN THE SHADE!"

LIKES:
STIRRING UP TROUBLE

DISLIKES:
BLENDING IN

PERSONALITY:
SHE'S A REAL SMOOTHIE OPERATOR!

DREAMS ABOUT:
HAVING SUPERPOWERS

QUOTE:
"LET'S MIX IT UP!"

BRENDA BLENDER

Toasty Pop

The only things warmer than Toasty Pop's personality are his words. When he gives a speech, there isn't a dry eye in the house.

HOBBIES:
THROWING PARTIES AND GIVING TOASTS

ISN'T AFRAID:
TO GRAB A SLICE OF LIFE

KNOWN FOR:
NEVER HAVING A STALE IDEA

BEST FRIEND:
BUTTERCUP

DISLIKES:
BURNING OUT

FAVORITE WEATHER:
DRY HEAT

QUOTE:

"Let's get cookin'!"

BEST FEATURE:
SHE'S NEVER AT A LOSS FOR WORDS!

PET PEEVE:
BUSY SIGNAL

FAVORITE GAME:
TELEPHONE

SECRET TALENT:
PUSHING PEOPLE'S BUTTONS

BEST FRIEND:
MOBILE MARY

Chatter

Chatter is dialed in to the latest gossip and loves to spread the word. Whether she's talking shop or just making chitchat, she always has a kind word for all her friends.

QUOTE:
"Call me!"

72

FROST T FRIDGE

PERSONALITY:
SUPER-CHILL

LIKES:
FEELING FULL!

FAVORITE WEATHER:
COLD AND CRISP

BAD HABIT:
LEAVING THE DOOR OPEN
AND THE LIGHTS ON

QUOTE:
"I'M KEEPIN' IT COOL!"

HOBBY:
CURLING UP WITH
A GOOD BOOK

PERSONALITY:
A BIG SOFTIE

**FAVORITE VACATION
DESTINATION:**
THE BIG EASY
(NEW ORLEANS)

FAVORITE GAME:
MUSICAL CHAIRS

QUOTE:
"LET'S GET ROCKING!"

COMFY CHAIR

GOOD AT:
GETTING IN TOUCH WITH
HER ROOTS

BIGGEST FEAR:
A FROSTY DAY

BEST FRIEND:
MINTEE

FASHION STYLE:
FLOWERS EVERYWHERE

FAVORITE COLOR:
VIOLET

FAVORITE VACATION
DESTINATION:
THE GARDEN STATE
(NEW JERSEY)

PETA PLANT

KNOWN FOR:
BRANCHING OUT AND
TRYING NEW THINGS

HOBBY:
WALKING IN THE WOODS

NICKNAME:
FIDDLEHEAD

FUTURE GOAL:
TURNING OVER
A NEW LEAF

QUOTE:
"WAY TO GROW!"

FREDA FERN

SPORTS SKILL:
CHANNEL SURFING

LIKES:
WHEN EVERYONE IS
LOOKING AT HER

BEST COSTUME:
RABBIT EARS

PERSONALITY:
PLUGGED IN

QUOTE:
"I'M ALL ABOUT
THE DRAMA!"

TAMMY TV

PENNY PENCIL

PERSONALITY:
HER HAPPINESS RUBS OFF
ON OTHERS.

HOBBIES:
WRITING AND DRAWING

NICKNAME:
NUMBER 2

BAD HABIT:
REACHING HER
BREAKING POINT

QUOTE:
"WRITE ON!"

KNOWN FOR:
PERFORMING MAGIC—
SHE LOVES TO MAKE
THINGS DISAPPEAR.

FAVORITE COLOR:
PINK

BEST FRIEND:
PENNY PENCIL

BAD HABIT:
SHE'S EASILY RUBBED
THE WRONG WAY.

LIKES:
NEW BEGINNINGS

ERICA ERASER

SECRET SALLY

PERSONALITY:
SHE'S PRETTY PRIVATE.

DISLIKES:
LOUDMOUTHS

GOOD AT:
REMEMBERING OLD TIMES

FAVORITE HOBBY:
PLAYING HIDE
AND SECRET

QUOTE:
"MY LIPS ARE SEALED!"

PENNY WISHING WELL

PERSONALITY:
SHE'S GOT BUCKETS
OF ENERGY.

COLLECTS:
COINS

GREATEST FEAR:
TROLLS

**FAVORITE VACATION
DESTINATION:**
THE TREVI FOUNTAIN

QUOTE:
"I WISH YOU WELL!"

PERSONALITY:
RELAXED

HOBBY:
SITTING IN THE
SUNSHINE

FAVORITE ANIMAL:
SONGBIRD

**FAVORITE
CHARACTER:**
WOODY WOODPECKER

QUOTE:
"TAKE IT EASY!"

WOODY GARDEN CHAIR

FAVORITE BOOK:
ANYTHING STEEPED
IN HISTORY

PET PEEVE:
SPOUTING NONSENSE

**FAVORITE SPORTS
TEAM:**
MILWAUKEE BREWERS

KNOWN FOR:
HAVING A HANDLE ON
ANY SITUATION

FAVORITE COLOR:
TEAL

POLLY TEAPOT

PERSONALITY:
FULL OF THE GOOD STUFF

**SIGNATURE DANCE
MOVE:**
JUG'S JIG

SPORTS SKILL:
SHE'S A GREAT TUMBLER.

BAD HABIT:
POURING IT ON THICK

QUOTE:
"YOU'RE PRETTY AS
A PITCHER!"

JEN JUG

PERSONALITY:
CHEERFUL

FAVORITE BOOK:
ANY TEARJERKER

BEST FRIEND:
JANE FRAME

KNOWN FOR:
ABSORBING OTHERS'
MOODS

QUOTE:
"DON'T CRY!"

TINY TISSUES

BERTHA BATH

PERSONALITY:
RUNS HOT AND COLD

PRIZED POSSESSION:
RUBBER DUCKIE

LIKES:
BLOWING BUBBLES

FAVORITE WEATHER:
SPRING RAIN SHOWERS

FAVORITE PRESIDENT:
WASHINGTON

♡ AISLE 8 ♡
LOOKIN' GOOD!

The health and beauty aisle is the place to be when you want to look—and feel!—good. The Shopkins here are always polished, but they know true beauty is found on the inside.

SPF 30+

HEALTH & BEAUTY

Lippy Lips

There's one word to describe this fashionista: beautiful. Lippy Lips lives to shop, loves to gab, and leaves her mark wherever she goes!

PERSONALITY: SASSY AND A BIT BOSSY

LIKES: GLOSSY MAGAZINES

STYLE SENSE: SHE HAS A DIFFERENT SHADE FOR EVERY MOOD.

DISLIKES: DULL COLORS

BEST FRIENDS: APPLE BLOSSOM AND POLLY POLISH

HOBBIES: ACTING AND SHOPPING

QUOTE:
"Have a beautiful day!"

Polly Polish

This stylish Shopkin is known for being a sharp dresser. She always looks put together and shines on any occasion!

PERSONALITY:
A RISK—TAKER

STYLE SENSE:
SHE LOVES TRYING NEW COLORS.

KNOWN FOR:
TELLING THE UNVARNISHED TRUTH

DISLIKES:
CHIPS

QUOTE:
"Nailed it!"

BEST FEATURE:
HIS PEARLY—WHITE SMILE

PRIZED POSSESSION:
A GOLDEN TOOTHBRUSH

FAVORITE COLOR:
MINT GREEN

FAVORITE STORYBOOK CHARACTER:
THE CHESHIRE CAT

Scrubs

Scrubs has the biggest smile of any Shopkin, especially when he's doing arts and crafts—he's a whiz with scissors and paste!

QUOTE:
"Keep on smiling!"

SHAMPY

PERSONALITY:
BUBBLY AND STYLISH

BAD HABIT:
GETTING WORKED UP
INTO A LATHER

FAVORITE WEATHER:
RAIN SHOWERS

BEST FEATURE:
SHE ALWAYS
SMELLS FRESH.

SIGNATURE DANCE
MOVE:
THE WAVE

PERSONALITY:
A SMOOTH OPERATOR

PET PEEVE:
A BAD HAIR DAY!

DISLIKES:
HOT WEATHER. IT MAKES
HER FEEL FRIZZY.

BEST FRIEND:
SHAMPY

LOVES:
SWIMMING AND
DAY SPAS

SILKY

Sunny Screen

Sunny Screen can be a bit of a worrier, but deep down she just wants to take care of her friends. No one's getting burned on her watch!

SPF 30+

FAVORITE VACATION DESTINATION:
MIAMI BEACH

FAVORITE WEATHER:
THE HOTTER THE BETTER!

PERFECT ACCESSORY:
HER SUNGLASSES, OF COURSE

FAVORITE COLOR:
ULTRAVIOLET

ENJOYS:
A COCONUT–BANANA SMOOTHIE

QUOTE:
"Life is a day at the beach!"

MINDY MIRROR

KNOWN FOR:
HER COMPACT SIZE

PERSONALITY:
REFLECTIVE AND
THOUGHTFUL

HERO:
SNOW WHITE

GREATEST FEAR:
SEVEN YEARS
OF BAD LUCK

QUOTE:
"HERE'S LOOKING
AT YOU!"

PERSONALITY:
A LITTLE CHEEKY

GOOD AT:
MAKING UP AFTER
A FIGHT

BEST FRIEND:
MINDY MIRROR

FAVORITE COLOR:
PINK

QUOTE:
"COLOR ME HAPPY!"

BLUSHY BRUSH

PERSONALITY:
A TRUE ROMANTIC

DREAM PET:
FRENCH BULLDOG

FASHION STYLE:
TRÉS CHIC!

FAVORITE VACATION
DESTINATION:
COLOGNE, FRANCE

QUOTE:
"OUI, OUI!"

LIMITED EDITION

FRENCHY PERFUME

LIMITED EDITION

GEMMA BOTTLE

PERSONALITY:
AB-SCENT MINDED

LIKES:
THE SWEET SMELL OF
SUCCESS

PRIZED POSSESSION:
CRYSTAL BALL

FAVORITE COLOR:
RAINBOW

KNOWN FOR:
HER FRAGRANT GARDEN

FAVORITE HOLIDAY:
MOTHER'S DAY

PERSONALITY:
LIGHT AND AIRY

DECORATING TIP:
PUT A BOW ON IT!

HOBBY:
MAKEOVERS AT
THE MALL

SECRET TALENT:
SNIFFING OUT A DEAL

PRETTY BOW KAY

PRETTY PUFF

HOBBY:
ENTERING BEAUTY
PAGEANTS

FAVORITE WEATHER:
MISTY

DREAMS ABOUT:
THE OCEAN SPRAY

QUOTE:
"I SMELL TROUBLE!"

PERSONALITY:
STRONG AND SWEET

BEST FRIEND:
CANDY KISSES

FAVORITE HOLIDAY:
VALENTINE'S DAY

LOVES READING:
ROMANCE NOVELS

BEST FEATURE:
HER NOSE FOR NEWS

SALLY SCENT

SPORTS SKILL:
PLAYING SHORT STOPPER

FAVORITE SONG:
"TWINKLE, TWINKLE,
LITTLE STAR"

HOBBY:
AROMATHERAPY

DREAMS ABOUT:
CATCHING LIGHTNING
IN A BOTTLE

BEST FEATURE:
EVERYONE TAKES A SHINE
TO HER.

SPARKLY SPRITZ

● AISLE 9 ●
SUPER STYLISH!

You can find all of the most fashionable Shopkins in the accessory aisle. They look great from head to toe because they know the real secret to style: a beautiful heart!

SHOES, HATS & ACCESSORIES

SIGNATURE DANCE MOVE:
THE BUNNY HOP

PRIZED POSSESSION:
LUCKY RABBIT'S FOOT

PERFECT ACCESSORY:
HER COZY BATHROBE

PERSONAL HERO:
THE EASTER BUNNY

QUOTE:
"I'LL GO TOE-TO-TOE WITH ANYONE!"

BUN BUN SLIPPER

SNEAKY WEDGE

PERSONALITY:
FOOTLOOSE AND FANCY-FREE

BAD HABIT:
LYING ABOUT HER HEIGHT

FAVORITE HANGOUT:
THE GYM

SECRET TALENT:
SHE CAN BE VERY SNEAKY.

PROMMY

LIKES:
GETTING DRESSED UP FOR SPECIAL OCCASSIONS

PERSONALITY:
HIGH–SPIRITED, NEVER FLAT

KNOWN FOR:
HER FABULOUS STYLE SENSE

HOBBY:
KICKING UP HER HEELS

QUOTE:
"YOU CAN NEVER LOOK TOO GORGEOUS!"

NICKNAME:
TOOTSIE

KNOWN FOR:
TAKING PROBLEMS IN STRIDE

PERSONALITY:
PRACTICAL, YET SLEEK

FAVORITE ACCESSORY:
LEG WARMERS

QUOTE:
"DON'T GO GETTING TOO BIG FOR YOUR BOOTS!"

LIMITED EDITION

ANGIE ANKLE BOOT

Sneaky Sally

Sneaky Sally is laced up and ready for action. She's got a competitive spirit and the sole of a champion.

SPORTS SKILL:
FANCY FOOTWORK

GOOD AT:
SOLVING KNOTTY PROBLEMS

LIKES:
BEING A STEP AHEAD OF HER FRIENDS

BEST FRIEND:
KELLY JELLY

DISLIKES:
UNSPORTING BEHAVIOR

BAD HABIT:
STICKING HER TONGUE OUT

QUOTE:
"If you don't try, you can't win!"

HEELY

SIGNATURE DANCE MOVE:
THE TWO-STEP

FAVORITE ANIMAL:
KITTEN

BEST FRIEND:
PROMMY

FAVORITE VACATION DESTINATION:
FASHION WEEK IN PARIS

QUOTE:
"I'LL KEEP YOU ON YOUR TOES!"

PERSONALITY:
A KID AT HEART

FAVORITE SPORT:
JELLY WRESTLING

BEST QUALITY:
BEING TOTALLY TRANSPARENT

SIGNATURE DANCE MOVE:
THE GRAPEVINE

QUOTE:
"DO I MAKE MYSELF CLEAR?"

KELLY JELLY

KNOWN FOR:
KEEPING EVERYONE IN STITCHES!

FAVORITE SONG:
"HEART AND SOLE"

SIGNATURE DANCE MOVE:
THE MOONWALK

PRIZED POSSESSION:
HER GRANDMOTHER'S QUILT

BEST FRIEND:
PENNY PURSE

FAVORITE MOVIE:
HAPPY FEET

Quilty Boot

Quilty Boot loves to dance up a storm! When she's not teaching the Shopkins all the latest steps, she's groovin' to the music she feels deep down in her sole!

QUOTE:
"These boots were made for walking!"

DISLIKES:
WET BLANKETS

FAVORITE HOBBY:
SPLASHING IN PUDDLES

BAD HABIT:
ALWAYS UP TO HER
ANKLES IN TROUBLE

FAVORITE COLOR:
YELLOW

QUOTE:
"WHATEVER YOU DO,
MAKE A SPLASH!"

JENNIFER RAYNE

TAYLOR RAYNE

PERSONALITY:
SLICKER THAN MOST

KNOWN FOR:
CHASING RAINBOWS!

BEST FRIEND:
HER SISTER, JENNIFER
RAYNE

SPORTS SKILL:
THE HAT TRICK

**SIGNATURE DANCE
MOVE:**
THE HEAD BOP

Casper Cap

Hat's off to Casper Cap! He can cap off any outfit and is always in peak condition. In fact, he's head and shoulders above the rest!

NICKNAME:
TEN-GALLON

DISLIKES:
HELMET HAIR

FAVORITE HOBBY:
BASEBALL

BEST FRIEND:
FLOPPY CAP

SECRET TALENT:
AM EXCELLENT BOWLER

FAVORITE VACATION DESTINATION:
PANAMA

QUOTE:
"Keep a lid on it!"

Handbag Harriet

Handbag Harriet is always prepared to handle anything. She's got all of life's necessities: money, snacks, tissues . . . and lots of laughs!

LIKES:
GETTING CARRIED AWAY

BAD HABIT:
KEEPING EVERYTHING INSIDE

DISLIKES:
EMPTY WALLETS

SPORTS SKILL:
CLUTCH SHOTS AT THE BUZZER

BEST FEATURE:
PURSED LIPS

NICKNAME:
POCKET BOOKWORM

QUOTE:

"I've got this in the bag!"

LIMITED EDITION

ROXY RING

PERSONALITY:
SPARKLING

HOBBY:
ATTENDING WEDDINGS

SIGNATURE DANCE MOVE:
THE FINGER TAP

FAVORITE COLOR:
SAPPHIRE BLUE

QUOTE:
"I'M A CUT ABOVE THE REST!"

LIKES:
ROCK BANDS

BEST FEATURE:
ALWAYS LOOKS FOR THE SILVER LINING

BEST FRIEND:
ROXY RING

FAVORITE COLOR:
RUBY RED

FAVORITE GAME:
RING-AROUND-THE-ROSY

LIMITED EDITION

RING-A-ROSIE

Ticky Tock

Things always run like clockwork with Ticky Tock around. It takes time to get to know her, but once you do the seconds will fly by.

PERSONALITY:
ORGANIZED AND PUNCTUAL

PET PEEVE:
RUNNING LATE

BEST FEATURE:
QUICK HANDS

FAVORITE HOBBY:
WATCHING TIME GO BY

FAVORITE POEM:
"HICKORY DICKORY DOCK"

BAD HABIT:
GETTING TOO WOUND UP

LIMITED EDITION

QUOTE:
"Time is on my side!"

KNOWN FOR:
BEING LUCKY

BEST FRIEND:
TICKY TOCK

FAVORITE FICTIONAL CHARACTER:
PRINCE CHARMING

FAVORITE HOBBY:
HANGING WITH HER BFF

FASHION STYLE:
HER OUTFITS ALWAYS MATCH.

DISLIKES:
BROKEN HEARTS

Chelsea Charm

Chelsea Charm lives a charmed life. Whether she's brightening up the day or just hanging around, she's a good friend who isn't afraid to show it!

QUOTE:
"Best Friends Forever!"

LIMITED EDITION

LIMITED EDITION

RUBY EARRING

PERSONALITY:
A DIAMOND IN THE ROUGH

FAVORITE COLOR:
EMERALD GREEN

BAD HABIT:
LEAVING HER FRIENDS DANGLING

SPORTS SKILL:
HANGING TEN

FAVORITE HOBBY:
GETTING HOOKED ON SOMETHING NEW

LIKES:
BEING WORN OUT

BEST FRIEND:
RUBY EARRING

KNOWN FOR:
THROWING DINNER PARTIES

FASHION STYLE:
NEAT AS A PIN

QUOTE:
"SHINE ON!"

LIMITED EDITION

BRENDA BROOCH

102

Penny Purse

She's always a tissue, a mirror, or a shoulder to lean on for all of her friends!

LIKES:
COINING NEW PHRASES

PET PEEVE:
GETTING STUCK WITH THE BILL

DISLIKES:
CHANGE

FAVORITE COLORS:
SILVER AND GOLD

HEROES:
ABRAHAM LINCOLN AND GEORGE WASHINGTON

FASHION STYLE:
POCKETS EVERYWHERE

QUOTE:
"My money's on you!"

ANIMAL INSTINCTS!

The Petkins aisle is the perfect place to find Shopkins' best friends. Whether they're learning new tricks or barking up the wrong tree, the Petkins are perfect animal companions!

PETKINS

Boneadette

Boneadette is one funny bone who's always yappy—except when she's buried by her dog friends.

FAVORITE HANGOUT:
THE BUTCHER SHOP

SPORTS SKILL:
THE DOGGY PADDLE

KNOWN FOR:
BITING OFF MORE THAN SHE CAN CHEW

HOBBY:
BIRD—WATCHING AND CHASING CARS

FAVORITE COLOR:
MILKY WHITE

FAVORITE WEATHER:
THE DOG DAYS OF SUMMER

DREAMS ABOUT:
BURIED TREASURE

FISH FLAKE JAKE

SIGNATURE DANCE MOVE:
THE SWIM

FAVORITE HOBBIES:
SWIMMING AND EATING

BEST FRIEND:
GOLDIE FISH BOWL

FAVORITE VEHICLE:
TANK

BAD HABIT:
FLAKING ON HIS HANDS

FAVORITE VACATION DESTINATION:
A DESERT ISLAND

BAD HABIT:
FALLING TO PIECES

FAVORITE HOLIDAY:
THE FOURTH OF JULY

PERSONALITY:
SWEET AND LOYAL—
A SHOPKIN YOU CAN
ALWAYS TRUST!

FASHION STYLE:
LOVES GINGHAM

SHY PIE

Hot Choc

Hot Choc is the purr-fect companion. This Petkin loves to play, but she also enjoys snuggling on cold, blustery days.

LIKES:
FAIRY TAILS

PERSONALITY:
WARM AND WELCOMING

DISLIKES:
CAT—ASTROPHES

BEST FEATURE:
HER SWEET PURR

BEST FRIEND:
MILK BUD

HERO:
COCO CHANEL

QUOTE:
"Meow!"

Milk Bud *

Milk Bud is a bundle of energy—and he really knows how to milk all the attention he can get!

FAVORITE HOBBY:
MAKING MOOSIC

LIKES:
CUDDLING

DISLIKES:
CURDLING

FAVORITE JOKE:
"WHAT DO YOU CALL A MAGICAL COW? THE DAIRY FAIRY!"

RITA REMOTE

PERSONALITY:
CONTROLLED

DISLIKES:
WHEN PEOPLE PUSH
HER BUTTONS

FAVORITE COLOR:
ANYTHING MUTED

KNOWN FOR:
CONSTANTLY CHANGING
HER TUNE

FAVORITE VACATION
DESTINATION:
THE ENGLISH CHANNEL

LIKES:
TAKING A CAT NAP

FAVORITE WEATHER:
POURING RAIN

FAVORITE COLOR:
GREEN

SIGNATURE DANCE
MOVE:
THE CANCAN

BAD HABIT:
SINKING HIS CLAWS IN

FAVORITE SONG:
"I'M A LITTLE TEAPOT"

DRIPS

♡ AISLE 11 ♡
TIME TO PLAY!

The talented Shopkins in this aisle are athletic, musical, and clever. They try their best, play to win, and always have fun. And with friends like these, playtime is always a home run!

SPORTS & ENTERTAINMENT

PERSONALITY:
READY FOR ACTION

NICKNAME:
LOUISVILLE SLUGGER

HALLOWEEN COSTUME:
VAMPIRE

SPORTS SKILL:
GRAND SLAM

QUOTE:
"GAME ON!"

GRACE BASEBALL BAT

KNOWN FOR:
STRIKING OUT ON HER OWN

FASHION STYLE:
SHE LIKES TO CHANGE IT UP.

NICKNAME:
SHORTSTOP

FAVORITE VACATION DESTINATION:
COOPERSTOWN, NEW YORK

QUOTE:
"LET'S PLAY BALL!"

BESSY BASEBALL

DENNIS BAT

KNOWN FOR:
MAKING A LOUD RACKET

FAVORITE ACCESSORY:
TENNIS SHOES

HERO:
SERENA WILLIAMS

DISLIKES:
BACKHANDED
COMPLIMENTS

QUOTE:
"LOVE IS JUST THE
BEGINNING!"

LIKES:
FEELING SAFE AT HOME

BEST FRIEND:
BESSY BASEBALL

HOBBY:
CATCHING SOME RAYS

DISLIKES:
STEALING

QUOTE:
"THREE STRIKES AND
YOU'RE OUT!"

BAILEY BASEBALL GLOVE

Lola Roller Blade

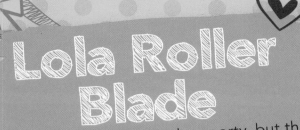

Lola Roller Blade may be sporty, but this athletic Shopkin never shoes-off—well, *almost* never! She'd rather roll through the park on a sunny day than compete one-on-one.

KNOWN FOR:
KEEPING HER FRIENDS INLINE

FAVORITE MUSIC:
ROCK 'N' ROLL

FAVORITE SONG:
"SKIDAMA–RINK"

NICKNAME:
DERBY DIVA!

BAD HABITS:
BEING A THIRD WHEEL

DISLIKES:
CHEAPSKATES

QUOTE:

"Let's roll!"

PERSONALITY:
SHE NEVER MISSES
A BEAT.

KNOWN FOR:
HER RHYTHM

LIKES:
PLAYING ALL
NIGHT LONG

DISLIKES:
POUNDING HEADACHES

SIGNATURE DANCE MOVE:
TAPPING

FAVORITE SONG:
"JINGLE BELLS"

Tammy Tambourine

Tammy Tambourine is a real mover and shaker. She may be a little loud, but when she puts her mind to something, she always does a bang-up job!

QUOTE:

"Let's band together and have some fun!"

POLLY PIANO

PERSONALITY:
KEYED-UP

FAVORITE COLORS:
BLACK AND WHITE

LUCKY NUMBER:
88

LIKES:
SHARP CHEDDAR

DISLIKES:
FLAT TIRES

PERSONALITY:
PLUCKY, YET COMPOSED

KNOWN FOR:
PULLING STRINGS TO GET
WHAT SHE WANTS

PRIZED POSSESSION:
HER NOTEBOOK

PET PEEVES:
CHEATS AND LYRES

QUOTE:
"THAT'S MUSIC TO
MY EARS!"

HILLARY HARP

Connie Console

Connie Console is quite competitive. She loves to push others' buttons and play games, but only if no one gets hurt!

PERSONALITY:
WIRED UP

NICKNAME:
R. CADE LOVER

FAVORITE ANIMAL:
DONKEY KONG

PET NAMES:
MARIO AND LUIGI

SPORTS SKILL:
X BOXING

QUOTE:
"With friends like the Shopkins, everyone wins!"

PERSONALITY:
MYSTERIOUS

KNOWN FOR:
FIGURING OUT TOUGH
PROBLEMS

HERO:
SHERLOCK HOLMES

BEST FRIEND:
CONNIE CONSOLE

QUOTE:
"WE CAN WORK
IT OUT!"

PAULA PUZZLE

LYNNE SPRING

PERSONALITY:
TIGHTLY WOUND UP

FAVORITE SONG:
"COILS JUST WANNA
HAVE FUN"

FASHION STYLE:
SLINKY AND COOL

**FAVORITE TIME
OF YEAR:**
MARCH, APRIL, AND MAY

NICKNAME:
STAIRMASTER

BELIEVES:
GREAT THINGS COME IN
SMALL PACKAGES.

FAVORITE ANIMAL:
TOY POODLE

HOBBY:
WALKING THE DOG

DREAMS ABOUT:
UNWINDING AT THE
END OF A LONG DAY

**SIGNATURE DANCE
MOVE:**
AROUND THE WORLD

BAD HABIT:
STRINGING OTHERS
ALONG

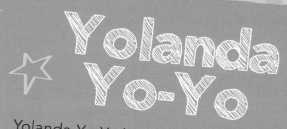

Yolanda Yo-Yo

Yolanda Yo-Yo knows that life has its ups and downs. But no matter how far away she travels, having friends like the Shopkins always helps her find the way back home.

COLLECTOR'S SHOPPING LIST

There are so many Shopkins to check out.
Use this list to collect the whole bunch!

CHECK OFF YOUR COLLECTED SHOPKINS TO SEE WHICH ONES YOU STILL HAVE TO FIND!

FINISHES:

GLITTER SHOPKINS

FROZEN SHOPKINS

METALLIC SHOPKINS

BLING SHOPKINS

FLUFFY BABY SHOPKINS

○ COMMON
○ RARE
○ ULTRA RARE
○ SPECIAL EDITION

Tommy Ketchup 1-015 ○	Nutty Butter 1-016 ●	Peppe Pepper 1-017 ○	Sally Shakes 1-018 ●
Sugar Lump 1-019 ○	Breaky Crunch 1-020 ●	Alpha Soup 1-021 ●	Gran Jam 1-022 ○
Coolio 1-023 ○	Tommy Ketchup 1-024 ●	Nutty Butter 1-025 ●	Peppe Pepper 1-026 ○
Sally Shakes 1-027 ●	Sugar Lump 1-028 ●	Breaky Crunch 1-029 ●	Alpha Soup 1-030 ○
Gran Jam 1-031 ○	Coolio 1-032 ○		

Fi Fi Flour 2-069 ●	Bart Beans 2-070 ○	Fasta Pasta 2-071 ○	Olivia Oil 2-072 ●
Honeeey 2-073 ●	Al Foil 2-074 ○	Toffy Coffee 2-075 ●	Cornell Mustard 2-076 ○
Chris P Crackers 2-077 ○	Fi Fi Flour 2-078 ●	Bart Beans 2-079 ○	Fasta Pasta 2-080 ●
Olivia Oil 2-081 ○	Honeeey 2-082 ●	Al Foil 2-083 ○	Toffy Coffee 2-084 ●
Cornell Mustard 2-085 ○	Chris P Crackers 2-086 ●		

120

:::::::SEASON 1::::::
****** FRUIT & VEG ******

Apple Blossom 1-001 ○	Rockin' Broc 1-002 ○	Strawberry Kiss 1-003 ●	Pineaple Crush 1-004 ○
Melonie Pips 1-005 ●	Miss Mushy Moo 1-006 ○	Posh Pear 1-007 ○	Apple Blossom 1-008 ○
Rockin' Broc 1-009 ○	Strawberry Kiss 1-010 ●	Pineapple Crush 1-011 ○	Melonie Pips 1-012 ●
Miss Musshy-Moo 1-013 ○	Posh Pear 1-014 ○		

::::::::SEASON 2::::::
****** FRUIT & VEG ******

Chloe Flower 2-001 ●	Sour Lemon 2-002 ●	Juicy Orange 2-003 ○	Corny Cob 2-004 ●
Garlic Rose 2-005 ○	Boo-Hoo Onion 2-006 ○	Dippy Avocado 2-007 ○	Silly Chilli 2-008 ○
Chloe Flower 2-009 ●	Sour Lemon 2-010 ●	Juicy Orange 2-011 ○	Corny Cob 2-012 ●
Garlic Rose 2-013 ○	Boo-Hoo Onion 2-014 ○	Dippy Avocado 2-015 ○	Silly Chilli 2-016 ○

SEASON 3
✱✱✱✱✱✱ FRUIT & VEG ✱✱✱✱✱✱✱

Peachy
3-069 ○

Wild
Carrot
3-070 ○

Sweet
Pea
3-071 ○

Pee Wee
Kiwi
3-072 ○

Aspara-
Gus
3-073 ●

Super
Celery
3-074 ●

Asbury
Raspberry
3-075 ○

Cherie
Tomatoe
3-076 ○

Peachy
3-077 ○

Wild
Carrot
3-078 ○

Sweet
Pea
3-079 ○

Pee Wee
Kiwi
3-080 ○

Aspara-
Gus
3-081 ●

Super
Celery
3-082 ○

Asbury
Raspberry
3-083 ○

Cherie
Tomatoe
3-084 ●

SEASON 4
✱✱✱✱✱✱ FRUIT & VEG ✱✱✱✱✱✱

Kris P
Lettuce
4-001 ○

Peely
Potato
4-002 ○

Milly
Mushroom
4-003 ○

Cheeky
Cherries
4-004 ○

April
Apricot
4-005 ●

Kris P
Lettuce
4-006 ○

Peely
Potato
4-007 ○

Milly
Mushroom
4-008 ○

Cheeky
Cherries
4-009 ○

April
Apricot
4-010 ●

SEASON 1
BAKERY

Bread Head 1-033 ○	Creamy Bun-Bun 1-034 ○	D'lish Donut 1-035 ●	Cheese Kate 1-036 ○
Mini Muffin 1-037 ○	Flutter Cake 1-038 ○	Kookie Cookie 1-039 ●	Bread Head 1-040 ○
Creamy Bun-Bun 1-041 ○	D'lish Donut 1-042 ●	Cheese Kate 1-043 ○	Mini Muffin 1-044 ○
Flutter Cake 1-045 ○	Kookie Cookie 1-046 ●		

SEASON 2
BAKERY

Slick Breadstick 2-035 ○	Mary Muffin 2-036 ●	Carrie Carrot Cake 2-037 ●	Mary Meringue 2-038 ●
Pecanna Pie 2-039 ●	Choco Lava 2-040 ○	Fifi Fruit Tart 2-041 ●	Danni Danish 2-042 ○
Cupcake Chic 2-043 ●	Slick Breadstick 2-044 ○	Mary Muffin 2-045 ●	Carrie Carrot Cake 2-046 ●
Mary Meringue 2-047 ●	Pecanna Pie 2-048 ●	Choco Lava 2-049 ○	Fifi Fruit Tart 2-050 ●
Danni Danish 2-051 ○	Cupcake Chic 2-052 ◍		

✱✱✱✱✱✱✱✱ BAKERY ✱✱✱✱✱✱✱✱

Cheese Louise 3-001	Queen of Tarts 3-002	Patty Cake 3-003	Lana Banana Bread 3-004
Toastie Bread 3-005	Candy Cookie 3-006	Birthday Betty 3-007	Wendy Wedding Cake 3-008
Nilla Slice 3-009	Cheese Louise 3-010	Queen of Tarts 3-011	Patty Cake 3-012
Lana Banana Bread 3-013	Toastie Bread 3-014	Candy Cookie 3-015	Birthday Betty 3-016
	Wendy Wedding Cake 3-017	Nilla Slice 3-018	

✱✱✱✱✱✱✱✱ BAKERY ✱✱✱✱✱✱✱✱

Bread Crumbs 4-011	Cookie Nut 4-012	Cindy Bon 4-013	Bagel Billy 4-014
Dolly Donut 4-015	Bread Crumbs 4-016	Cookie Nut 4-017	Cindy Bon 4-018
	Bagel Billy 4-019	Dolly Donut 4-020	

✱✱✱✱✱✱✱ DAIRY ✱✱✱✱✱✱✱

Chee Zee 1-065	Swiss Miss 1-066	Spilt Milk 1-067	Ghurty 1-068
○	○	●	●
Millie Shake 1-069	**Flava Ava 1-070**	**Dollops 1-071**	**Googy 1-072**
●	○	○	○
Chee Zee 1-073	**Swiss Miss 1-074**	**Spilt Milk 1-075**	**Ghurty 1-076**
○	○	●	●
Millie Shake 1-077	**Flava Ava 1-078**	**Dollops 1-079**	**Googy 1-080**
●	○	○	○

✱✱✱✱✱✱✱✱ FROZEN ✱✱✱✱✱✱✱✱

Ice Cream Dream 1-121	Popsi Cool 1-122	Yo-Chi 1-123	Cool Cube 1-124
●	○	●	●
Pa' Pizza 1-125	**Snow Crush 1-126**	**Fishtix 1-127**	**Freezy Peazy 1-128**
○	○	○	○
Ice Cream Dream 1-129	**Popsi Cool 1-130**	**Yo-Chi 1-131**	**Cool Cube 1-132**
○	○	○	○
Pa' Pizza 1-133	**Snow Crush 1-134**	**Fishtix 1-135**	**Freezy Peazy 1-136**
○	○	○	○

SEASON 2
*** CLEANING & LAUNDRY ***

Dishy Liquid 2-087 ○	Squeaky Clean 2-088 ○	Wendy Washer 2-089 ●	Bree Freshner 2-090 ○
Molly Mops 2-091 ●	Sweeps 2-092 ●	Sarah Softner 2-093 ○	Peta Plunger 2-094 ●
Leafy 2-095 ○	Dishy Liquid 2-096 ○	Squeaky Clean 2-097 ●	Wendy Washer 2-098 ●
Bree Freshner 2-099 ○	Molly Mops 2-100 ●	Sweeps 2-101 ●	Sarah Softner 2-102 ○
	Peta Plunger 2-103 ●	Leafy 2-104 ○	

SEASON 2
******** BABY ********

Dribbles 2-121 ●	Ga Ga Gourmet 2-122 ○	Dum Mee Mee 2-123 ●	Baby Swipes 2-124 ●
Sippy Sips 2-125 ●	Baby Puff 2-126 ○	Nappy Dee 2-127 ●	Shampoo Sue 2-128 ○
Dribbles 2-129 ○	Ga Ga Gourmet 2-130 ○	Dum Mee Mee 2-131 ●	Baby Swipes 2-132 ●
Sippy Sips 2-133 ●	Baby Puff 2-134 ○	Nappy Dee 2-135 ●	Shampoo Sue 2-136 ●

SEASON 4 : PETSHOP

Doggy Bowl 4-073	Little Pet Collar 4-074	Dennis Ball 4-075	Pup-E-House 4-076
Kitty Catbed 4-077	Teena Catfood 4-078	Goldie Fish Bowl 4-079	Pup E Brush 4-080
Doggy Bowl 4-081	Little Pet Collar 4-082	Dennis Ball 4-083	Pup-E-House 4-084
Kitty Catbed 4-085	Teena Catfood 4-086	Goldie Fish Bowl 4-087	Pup E Brush 4-088

SEASON 2 : HOMEWARES

Toasty Pop 2-017	Brenda Blender 2-018	Coffee Drip 2-019	Saucy Pan 2-020
Ma Kettle 2-021	Zappy Microwave 2-022	Lisa Litter 2-023	Lana Lamp 2-024
Sizzles 2-025	Toasty Pop 2-026	Brenda Blender 2-027	Coffee Drip 2-028
Saucy Pan 2-029	Ma Kettle 2-030	Zappy Microwave 2-031	Lisa Litter 2-032
Lana Lamp 2-033	Sizzles 2-034		

SEASON 3
★★★★★★ HOMEWARES ★★★★★

Washa 3-103	Vicky Vac 3-104	Frost T Fridge 3-105	Blow-Anne 3-106
Teenie TV 3-107	Radio Sue 3-108	Chatter 3-109	Mobile Mary 3-110
Mixie & Maxie 3-111	Washa 3-112	Vicky Vac 3-113	Frost T Fridge 3-114
Blow-Anne 3-115	Teenie TV 3-116	Radio Sue 3-117	Chatter 3-118
	Mobile Mary 3-119	Mixie & Maxie 3-120	

SEASON 4
★★★★★★ HOMEWARES ★★★★★★

Edgar Eggcup 4-041	Comfy Chair 4-042	Tammy TV 4-043	Gale Scales 4-044
Flushes 4-045	Edgar Eggcup 4-046	Comfy Chair 4-047	Tammy TV 4-048
	Gale Scales 4-049	Flushes 4-050	

SEASON 1
SWEET TREATS

Bubbles 1-047	Candy Kisses 1-048	Le'Quorice 1-049	Cheeky Chocolate 1-050
Candi Cotton 1-051	Lolli Poppins 1-052	Mandy Candy 1-053	Jelly B 1-054
Miss Twist 1-055	Bubbles 1-056	Candy Kisses 1-057	Le'Quorice 1-058
Cheeky Chocolate 1-059	Candi Cotton 1-060	Lolli Poppins 1-061	Mandy Candy 1-062
	Jelly B 1-063	Miss Twist 1-064	

SEASON 2
SWEET TREATS

Poppy Corn 2-053	Minnie Mintie 2-054	Banana Splitty 2-055	Yummy Gum 2-056
Waffle Sue 2-057	Ice Cream Dream 2-058	Cheery Churro 2-059	Pamela Pancake 2-060
Poppy Corn 2-061	Minnie Mintie 2-062	Banana Splitty 2-063	Yummy Gum 2-064
Waffle Sue 2-065	Ice Cream Dream 2-066	Cheery Churro 2-067	Pamela Pancake 2-068

PopRock 3-051 ○

Cream E Cookie 3-052 ○

Macca Roon 3-053 ○

Chocky Box 3-054 ○

Wanda Wafer 3-055 ○

Choc Kiss 3-056 ○

Suzie Sundae 3-057 ○

Candy Apple 3-058 ○

Ginger Fred 3-059 ○

PopRock 3-060 ○

Cream E Cookie 3-061 ○

Macca Roon 3-062 ○

Chocky Box 3-063 ○

Wanda Wafer 3-064 ○

Choc Kiss 3-065 ○

Suzie Sundae 3-066 ○

Candy Apple 3-067 ○

Ginger Fred 3-068 ○

Ice Cream Queen 4-021 ○

Jiggly Jelly 4-022 ○

Pancake Jake 4-023 ○

Berry Smoothie 4-024 ○

Betsy Buttercup 4-025 ○

Ice Cream Queen 4-026 ○

Jiggly Jelly 4-027 ○

Pancake Jake 4-028 ○

Berry Smoothie 4-029 ○

Betsy Buttercup 4-030 ○

130

SEASON 1
★★★★★★ PARTY FOOD ★★★★★

Crispy Chip 1-081 ○	Pretz-elle 1-082 ○	Wobbles 1-083 ○	Rainbow Bite 1-084 ○
Wishes 1-085 ●	Frank Furter 1-086 ○	Little Sipper 1-087 ○	Fairy Crumbs 1-088 ○
Cheezy B 1-089 ●	Soda Pops 1-090 ●	Crispy Chip 1-091 ○	Pretz-elle 1-092 ○
Wobbles 1-093 ○	Rainbow Bite 1-094 ○	Wishes 1-095 ○	Frank Furter 1-096 ○
Little Sipper 1-097 ○	Fairy Crumbs 1-098 ○	Cheezy B 1-099 ●	Soda Pops 1-100 ●

SEASON 4
★★★★★★★ PARTY TIME ★★★★★★★

Miss Pressy 4-063 ○	Mary Wishes 4-064 ○	Marty Party Hat 4-065 ○	June Balloon 4-066 ○
Party Plate 4-067 ○	Miss Pressy 4-068 ○	Mary Wishes 4-069 ○	Marty Party Hat 4-070 ○
	June Balloon 4-071 ○	Party Plate 4-072 ○	

SEASON 1
✳✳✳ HEALTH & BEAUTY ✳✳✳

Scrubs
1-101

Lippy
Lips
1-102

Curly
1-103

Shampy
1-104

Silky
1-105

Bubble
Tubs
1-106

Chap-
Elli
1-107

Polly
Polish
1-108

Suds
1-109

Toofs
1-110

Scrubs
1-111

Lippy
Lips
1-112

Curly
1-113

Shampy
1-114

Silky
1-115

Bubble
Tubs
1-116

Chap-
Elli
1-117

Polly Polish
1-118

Subs
1-119

Toofs
1-120

SEASON 3
✳✳✳✳✳✳ STATIONERY ✳✳✳✳✳✳

Stella
Stapler
3-121

Snippy
3-122

Penny
Pencil
3-123

Noni
Notebook
3-124

Erica
Eraser
3-125

Kelly
Calculator
3-126

Rita
Ruler
3-127

Secret
Sally
3-128

Stella
Stapler
3-129

Snippy
3-130

Penny
Pencil
3-131

Noni
Notebook
3-132

Erica
Eraser
3-133

Kelly
Calculator
3-134

Rita
Ruler
3-135

Secret
Sally
3-136

::::::::::::SEASON 2::::::::::
******* SHOES *******

Prommy 2-105	Sneaky Sue 2-106	Heels 2-107	Sneaky Wedge 2-108
Betty Boot 2-109	Wedgy Wendy 2-110	Bun Bun Slipper 2-111	Cute Boot 2-112
Prommy 2-113	Sneaky Sue 2-114	Heels 2-115	Sneaky Wedge 2-116
Betty Boot 2-117	Wedgy Wendy 2-118	Bun Bun Slipper 2-119	Cute Boot 2-120

:::::::::::SEASON 3:::::::::::
******** SHOES ********

Beverley Heels 3-035	Shoes-Anne 3-036	Jennifer Rayne 3-037	Molly Moccasin 3-038
Lizzy Lace-up 3-039	Sneaky Sally 3-040	Snug Ugg 3-041	Wilma Wedge 3-042
Beverley Heels 3-043	Shoes-Anne 3-044	Jennifer Rayne 3-045	Molly Moccasin 3-046
Lizzy Lace-up 3-047	Sneaky Sally 3-048	Snug Ugg 3-049	Wilma Wedge 3-050

SEASON 3
HATS

Casper Cap 3-019

Hattie Hat 3-020

Flappy Cap 3-021

Brimmy 3-022

Toni Topper 3-023

Shady 3-024

Bonnie Beret 3-025

Taylor Rayne 3-026

Casper Cap 3-027

Hattie Hat 3-028

Flappy Cap 3-029

Brimmy 3-030

Toni Topper 3-031

Shady 3-032

Bonnie Beret 3-033

Taylor Rayne 3-034

SEASON 4
ACCESSORIES

Sharon Shoe 4-031

Handbag Harriet 4-032

Wooly Hat 4-033

Jules 4-034

Sasha Belt 4-035

Sharon Shoe 4-036

Handbag Harriet 4-037

Wooly Hat 4-038

Jules 4-039

Sasha Belt 4-040

:SEASON 3:
*** INTERNATIONAL FOOD ***

Suzie Sushi 3-085	Humpty Dumpling 3-086	Lammy Lamington 3-087	Netti Spaghetti 3-088
Croissant d'Or 3-089	Fiona Fries 3-090	Sconnie 3-091	Taco Terrie 3-092
Sausage Sizzle 3-093	Suzie Sushi 3-094	Humpty Dumpling 3-095	Lammy Lamington 3-096
Netti Spaghetti 3-097	Croissant d'Or 3-098	Fiona Fries 3-099	Sconnie 3-100
	Taco Terrie 3-101	Sausage Sizzle 3-102	

:SEASON 4:
******** GARDEN ********

Peta Plant 4-051	Tiny Tree 4-052	Will Barrow 4-053	Prickles 4-054
Pheobe Fork 4-055	Mintee 4-056	Peta Plant 4-057	Tiny Tree 4-058
Will Barrow 4-059	Prickles 4-060	Pheobe Fork 4-061	Mintee 4-062

135

Jilly Jam 4-089	Tracey Tomato 4-090	Shy Pie 4-091	Jilly Jam 4-092

Tracey Tomato 4-093	Shy Pie 4-094	Milk Bud 4-095	Tubby Butter 4-096

Hot Choc 4-097	Milk Bud 4-098	Tubby Butter 4-099	Hot Choc 4-100

Big Topping 4-101	Mabel Syrup 4-102	Ice Cream Cup 4-103	

Big Topping 4-104	Mabel Syrup 4-105	Ice Cream Cup 4-106	

Bobby Sock 4-107	Jingle Purse 4-108	Earring Twins 4-109	

Bobby Sock 4-110	Jingle Purse 4-111	Earring Twins 4-112	

Eggchic 4-113	Comfy Cushion 4-114	Rita Remote 4-115	Eggchic 4-116

Comfy Cushion 4-117	Rita Remote 4-118	Drips 4-119	Burt House 4-120

Jade Spade 4-121	Drips 4-122	Burt House 4-123	Jade Spade 4-124

Bone-adette 4-125	Waggy Tag 4-126	Fish Flake Jake 4-127	Bone-adette 4-128

Waggy Tag 4-129	Fish Flake Jake 4-130	Dinky Drink 4-131	Flicker Candle 4-132

Whistle Wilma 4-133	Dinky Drink 4-134	Flicker Candle 4-135	Whistle Wilma 4-136

Cupcake Queen 1-137	Buttercup 1-138	Tin'a' Tuna 1-139	Twinky Winks 1-140

Papa Tomato 1-141	Sunny Screen 1-142

Marsha Mellow 2-137	Rub-a-Glove 2-138	Lenny Lime 2-139	Lee Tea 2-140

Donna Donut 2-141	Angie Ankle Boot 2-142

Ruby Earring 3-137	Chelsea Charm 3-138	Ring-A-Rosie 3-139	Ticky Tock 3-140

Brenda Brooch 3-141	Roxy Ring 3-142

Frenchy Perfume 4-137	Pretty Puff 4-138	Sparkly Spritz 4-139	Pretty Bow Kay 4-140

Gemma Bottle 4-141	Sally Scent 4-142

SEASON 5 CHARMS

Lippy Lips 5-097	Kooky Cookie 5-098	Cupcake Chic 5-099	D'Lish Donut 5-100
Prommy 5-101	Strawberry Kiss 5-102	Cheeky Chocolate 5-103	Spilt Milk 5-104
Yo-Chi 5-105	Dum Mee Mee 5-106	Polly Polish 5-107	Apple Blossom 5-108
Lippy Lips 5-109	Kooky Cookie 5-110	Cupcake Chic 5-111	D'Lish Donut 5-112

SEASON 5 CHARMS

Prommy 5-113	Strawberry Kiss 5-114	Cheeky Chocolate 5-115	Spilt Milk 5-116
Yo-Chi 5-117	Dum Mee Mee 5-118	Polly Polish 5-119	Apple Blossom 5-120
Lippy Lips 5-121	Kooky Cookie 5-122	Cupcake Chic 5-123	D'Lish Donut 5-124
Prommy 5-125	Strawberry Kiss 5-126	Cheeky Chocolate 5-127	Spilt Milk 5-128
Yo-Chi 5-129	Dum Mee Mee 5-130	Polly Polish 5-131	Apple Blossom 5-132

SEASON 5
GARDEN

Woody Garden Chair 5-017	Walter Watering Can 5-018	Penny Wishing Well 5-019	Winnie Window Box 5-020

Barb B Que 5-021	Freda Fern 5-022	Launa Mower 5-023	Peta Planter 5-024

Woody Garden Chair 5-025	Walter Watering Can 5-026	Penny Wishing Well 5-027	Winnie Window Box 5-028

Barb B Que 5-029	Freda Fern 5-030	Launa Mower 5-031	Peta Planter 5-032

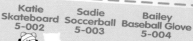

SEASON 5
SPORT

Dennis Bat 5-001	Katie Skateboard 5-002	Sadie Soccerball 5-003	Bailey Baseball Glove 5-004

Grace Baseball Bat 5-005	Lola Roller Blade 5-006	Bessy Baseball 5-007	Snorky 5-008

Dennis Bat 5-009	Katie Skateboard 5-010	Sadie Soccerball 5-011	Bailey Baseball Glove 5-012

Grace Baseball Bat 5-013	Lola Roller Blade 5-014	Bessy Baseball 5-015	Snorky 5-016

139

::::::::::SEASON 5::::::::::
********** **BAKERY** **********

Brittney Brownie 6-065	Dolly Donut 5-066	Ollie Orange Cake 5-067	Mel T Moment 5-068
○	○	○	○

Jilly Jam Roll 5-069	Creamy Cookie Cupcake 5-070	Linda Layered Cake 5-071	Royal Cupcake 5-072
○	○	○	○

Brittney Brownie 5-073	Dolly Donut 5-074	Ollie Orange Cake 5-075	Mel T Moment 5-076
○	○	○	○

Jilly Jam Roll 5-077	Creamy Cookie Cupcake 5-078	Linda Layered Cake 5-079	Royal Cupcake 5-080
○	○	○	○

::::::::::SEASON 5::::::::::
********** **TECH** **********

Percy P.C 5-133	Sammy Speaker 5-134	Clicky Mouse 5-135	Gabby Gamer 5-136
○	○	○	○

Cam Corder 5-137	Lizzy Laptop 5-138	Howard Powerboard 5-139	Connie Console 5-140
○	○	○	○

Percy P.C 5-141	Sammy Speaker 5-142	Clicky Mouse 5-143	Gabby Gamer 5-144
○	○	○	○

Cam Corder 5-145	Lizzy Laptop 5-146	Howard Powerboard 5-147	Connie Console 5-148
○	○	○	○

Rockin' Choc 5-081	Cute Fruit Jello 5-082	Sprinkle Lee Cake 5-083	Mandy Mousse 5-084
○	●	○	○

Ice Cream Kate 5-085	Cuppa Cocoa 5-086	Chocky Croissant 5-087	Tasty Toast 5-088
○	○	○	○

Rockin' Choc 5-089	Cute Fruit Jello 5-090	Sprinkle Lee Cake 5-091	Mandy Mousse 5-092
○	●	○	○

Ice Cream Kate 5-093	Cuppa Cocoa 5-094	Chocky Croissant 5-095	Tasty Toast 5-096
○	○	○	○

Claire Chair 5-049	Jane Frame 5-050	Bertha Bath 5-051	Tiny Tissues 5-052
●	●	○	○

Veronica Vase 5-053	Jen Jug 5-054	Polly Teapot 5-055	Lynn Lamp 5-056
○	●	●	○

Claire Chair 5-057	Jane Frame 5-058	Bertha Bath 5-059	Tiny Tissues 5-060
○	○	○	○

Veronica Vase 5-061	Jen Jug 5-062	Polly Teapot 5-063	Lynn Lamp 5-064
○	●	○	○

SEASON 5
********** MUSIC **********

Plucky Guitar 5-033 ○

Fun Drum 5-034 ○

Polly Piano 5-035 ○

Tammy Tambourine 5-036 ○

Mike Rophone 5-037 ○

Khia Board 5-038 ○

Hillary Harp 5-039 ○

Max Saxophone 5-040 ○

Plucky Guitar 5-041 ○

Fun Drum 5-042 ○

Polly Piano 5-043 ○

Tammy Tambourine 5-044 ○

Mike Rophone 5-045 ○

Khia Board 5-046 ○

Hillary Harp 5-047 ○

Max Saxophone 5-048 ○

SEASON 5
***** LIMITED EDITION *****

Paula Puzzle 5-149 ●

Fortune Stella 5-150 ●

Lynne Spring 5-151 ●

Yolanda Yo-Yo 5-152 ●

Blocky 5-153 ●

Spinderella 5-154 ●

BREAKFAST

SCRAMBLED EGGS

Betsy Butter 6-001 + Shelly Egg 6-002 + Melissa Milk 6-003 + Toast T. Warm 6-031

Polly Parsley 6-032 + Small-Fry Pan 6-067 = Sami Scrambles 6-049

STRAWBERRY PANCAKES

Shelly Egg 6-002 + Melissa Milk 6-003 + Fleur Flour 6-004 + Strawberry Top 6-005

Mavis Maple Syrup 6-068 = Berry Sweet Pancakes 6-050

BANANA SMOOTHIE

Melissa Milk 6-003 + Runny Honey 6-008 + V. Nilla Tubs 6-012 + Buncho Bananas 6-013

Blocky Ice Cube 6-033 + P. Nut Butter 6-070 = Briana Banana Smoothie 6-053

WAFFLES & RASPBERRIES

Melissa Milk 6-003 + Fleur Flour 6-004 + Kane Sugar 6-009 + Ros Berry 6-034

Olive Oil 6-035 = Winona Waffles 6-054

LEMON & HONEY TEA

Runny Honey 6-008 + Kane Sugar 6-009 + Herb L. Teabag 6-010

Pippa Lemon 6-011 + = Tegan Tea 6-052

SAUSAGE EGG MUFFIN

Shelly Egg 6-002 + Madeline Muffin 6-006 + Charlie Cheese 6-007

Susie Sausage 6-069 = Barbie Breakfast Muffin 6-051

CHECK OUT THE SEASON 6 SHOPKINS

FOR AN EXTRA SPECIAL SURPRISE: COLLECT AS MANY AS YOU CAN TO **CREATE YOUR OWN DELICIOUS RECIPES**

SEASON 6 FINISHES:

- DAZZLING SHOPKINS
- GLITTER SHOPKINS
- COLOR CHANGE SHOPKINS

CUPCAKE PRINCESS   **BAKERY**

Betsy Butter 6-001 + Shelly Egg 6-002 + Melissa Milk 6-003 + Fleur Flour 6-004

Cassie Caster Sugar 6-040 + Freda Frosting 6-073 = Cupcake Princess 6-058

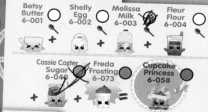

COOKIES

Betsy Butter 6-001 + Shelly Egg 6-002 + Fleur Flour 6-004 + Kane Sugar 6-009

Choc Chips 6-014 + Vicki Vanilla 6-036 + Dusty Cocoa 6-071 = Stacks Cookie 6-055

CARROT CAKE

Shelly Egg 6-002 + Fleur Flour 6-004 + Karen Carrot 6-015 + Vicki Vanilla 6-036

Iris Icing Sugar 6-037 + Cassie Caster Sugar 6-040 + Goldie Syrup 6-072 = Cara Carrot Cake 6-056

APPLE PIE

Betsy Butter 6-001 + Melissa Milk 6-003 + Fleur Flour 6-004 + Adam Apple 6-038

Cinnamon Sally 6-039 + = Apple Pie Alice 6-057

143

SPAGHETTI BOLOGNESE   **FAMILY FOOD**

Roma Tomato 6-021 + Patsy Pasta 6-022 + C.Salt 6-023 + Teary Onion 6-024

Parmesan Pete 6-043 + Bridie Basil 6-075 = Twirly Spaghetti 6-061

VEGGIE PIZZA

Button Mushroom 6-016 + Pappa Pizza Base 6-019 + Timmy Tomato Paste 6-020 + Bella Mozzarella 6-042

Olivia Olive 6-074 = Veronica Veggie Pizza 6-060

HONEY SOY NOODLES

Runny Honey 6-008 + Button Mushroom 6-016 + Sam Soy 6-017 + Bethany Broccoli 6-018

Nina Noodles 6-041 = Natalie Noodles 6-059

FRIED RICE

Karen Carrot 6-015 + Button Mushroom 6-016 + Sam Soy 6-017 + Jasmine Rice 6-025

Sweet Corn 6-026 + Olive Oil 6-035 + Chili Peppa 6-044 = Freddy Fried Rice 6-062

BANANA SPLIT   **SWEETS**

V. Nilla Tubs 6-012 + Buncho Bananas 6-013 + Miss Sprinkles 6-029 + Little Choc Bottle 6-030

Wilbur Whipped Cream 6-047 + Carmel Topping 6-048 + Wanda Wafer 7-078 + B. Nana Split 6-065

CHOCOLATE SUNDAE

Choc Chips 6-014 + Choc E. Tubs 6-027 + Miss Sprinkles 6-029 + Little Choc Bottle 6-030

Wilbur Whipped Cream 6-047 = Choc-Kate Sundae 6-066

HONEYCOMB ICE CREAM CAKE

Choc Chips 6-014 + Choc E. Tubs 6-027 + Berry Tubs 6-045 + Cherry-Anne 6-046

Harvey Honeycomb 6-076 = Sweets Honey 6-063

ICE CREAM SANDWICH

V. Nilla Tubs 6-012 + Choc Chips 6-014 + Choc N' Chip 6-028 + Miss Sprinkles 6-029

Choc Buds 7-077 + Freezy Bites 6-064

LIMITED EDITION
CUTETENSILS

Tiny Tiara Topper 7-079 + Patricia Parfait Glass 7-080 + Belinda Blender 7-081 + Bessie Bowl 7-082

Pizza Will 7-083 + Whitney Whisk 7-084 + Patty Case 7-085 + Judy Jug 7-086

🥄 STAPLE INGREDIENTS
(SHOPKINS FEATURED IN MORE THAN ONE RECIPE)